Understanding Child Behaviour

Understanding Child Behaviour

Rob Long

Quay Books
in association with
MA Education Limited

Quay Books Division, MA Education Limited, Jesses Farm, Snow Hill,
Dinton, Salisbury Wiltshire, SP3 5HN

British Library Cataloguing-in-Publication Data
A catalogue record is available for this book

© MA Education Limited 2004
ISBN 1 85642 272 0

Reprinted 2004

Printed in the UK by Cromwell Press, Trowbridge

Contents

Foreword

Children are not adults. The changes that children successfully pass through enable them to become adults with coping skills to face the challenges that they will inevitably meet. They change physically, behaviourally, emotionally, cognitively and socially. As these changes are taking place they are developing both a sense of personal identity as well as their self-esteem. During these early formative years, children can meet challenges that are beyond their existing coping skills. This is when problems can arise. Each of the chapters in this book, explores key themes of behaviour, the playground, resiliency and stress as well as exploring such central skills as listening. It is written for the practitioner working with young children who wishes both to reinforce their existing skills and extend their understanding.

Rob Long
November, 2003

1

Making sense of behaviour

The more we understand children's behaviour, the more difficult
it can seem to make sense of why they do what they do — it is
complicated. Throughout history, people have written how
impossible children are to control. Evidence today suggests that
there is an increase in challenging/difficult behaviour. The term
most commonly used today is that children face emotional,
behavioural and social difficulties. In the past we have not
included social. This is strange because it is in a social context
that we observe such difficulties.

Understanding emotional, behavioural and social difficulties (EBSD)

There is no, and never can be a fixed definition of 'emotional,
behavioural and social difficulties'. Its meaning varies between
observers and across time and place. How we each understand
any specific behaviour will depend upon its frequency, duration,
intensity, abnormality and effect on us and others. The
behaviour we are concerned with is on a continuum between
behaviour which may concern us, but is within normal limits, to
behaviour which is extreme, requiring more specialist support.

Our concern is with behaviour which has become a barrier to
a child being able to learn. The reasons for this can be many: it
may be the result of stress/distress, or the pupil having failed to

learn the appropriate rules, or through their seemingly choosing wilfully to refuse to comply with reasonable adult requests.

Before a child arrives in school there are many 'at risk factors' that they may either possess or have experienced. At risk means that they increase the possibility of a child developing EBSD. It does not mean that there is an inevitability to it.

What are the 'at risk' factors: a multi-factorial model

In a child:

- low self-esteem
- bereavement
- family breakdown
- learning difficulties
- physical difference
- temperament
- ethnic background
- physical, visual, auditory impairment
- being physically more or less mature than peers.

In the family:

- inconsistent parenting
- over-indulgent parenting
- serial parenting
- child as carer to parent
- mental illness

- physical, sexual, emotional abuse
- alcohol abuse
- drug abuse
- over-crowding
- sibling rivalry
- step-children conflict
- anti-educational attitude
- poverty
- unemployment
- family breakdown
- bereavement.

In the community:

- poor housing
- lack of resources
- racist community
- anti-religious tolerance
- community disputes
- drug culture
- peer pressure.

The younger a child begins to show EBSD, the cause is likely to be the interplay between at-home factors and the child's personality. When EBSD emerge during adolescence — often at secondary school — then the key factors are peer influence, status frustration, combined with personality/identity issues.

Early 'at risk' factors can set the stage for later ones to have an increased influence. The reasons why such behaviours develop are many; they may be the result of stress/distress or the pupil having failed to learn the appropriate rules.

It is not hard to see that many children enter school with many at risk factors operating in their lives. Each of these factors contribute towards an increased likelihood of their developing EBSD; when there is a cocktail effect, the probability must be greatly increased. Evidence also supports the view that there are definite steps towards EBSD. Children usually pass through A to get to B: children develop minor EBSD before they develop serious ones.

Multi pathways

EBSD are usually the result of a conglomeration of factors added together, some combinations being far more potent than others. Similarly, there will be different developmental pathways to different types of EBSD.

The behaviour that is giving cause for concern may be a 'conduct disorder', or an 'emotional/mood disorder'. The two are often inter-related, though the conduct disorders are naturally more noticeable on account of their effect on other pupils and the teacher.

Children with emotional and behavioural difficulties are usually:

- unhappy, unwilling and/or unable
- achieve less praise through their work
- have fewer positive adult interactions
- have learning difficulties or are under-achieving
- have poor social skills and few friends
- have a poor self-regard
- are emotionally volatile
- are easily hurt, upset by others.

It is clear that no single cause cause exists to explain children's EBSD. But, there are some that seem to be more readily understandable. For example, a child who is grieving the loss of a parent may become aggressive and challenging. Many children who display emotional and behavioural difficulties often have experienced some form of stress. At other times, the causes are perplexing and not readily identifiable. We do not always need to know the causes to be able to decide ways of supporting the child, and prevent their difficulties from worsening.

Children with emotional and behavioural difficulties face disabilities which prevent them from learning.

Most children with emotional and behavioural difficulties respond well to suitable in-school programmes.

To help support children who face EBSD there are some key questions that need to be explored: these lead to key principles that can help guide our actions.

Personal awareness increases personal control

Why do I find some children harder to manage than others?

Why is it that some children seem to 'hit my buttons', while with others I can stay calm and manage their behaviour easily? We each carry emotional memories from our childhood, similar to how certain odours can trigger off past memories. This explains why we can take an immediate liking to some people but not to others. But have you noticed sometimes that you do not get on with people you expect to like and vice versa. Well, it is similar with children, some children trigger off good feelings.

This means that while their behaviour is difficult and challenging, we can stay calm when managing them. But, the child that unwittingly 'hits our buttons' is the one with whom we need to work harder to stop our own emotional memories colouring our reaction.

So what can you do?

When such children are difficult to manage try some of these everyday techniques. Stop and:

- count to ten
- give the child an option and come back in five minutes
- practise breathing slowly and deeply
- try to see the situation from the child's viewpoint
- reframe the situation — what is the child trying to achieve?
- do not personalise issues, look for reasons
- talk with colleagues
- develop a plan of action.

Remember, the children you find hard to manage are the ones that are enabling you to develop new skills. Once you can manage them, well, you may find that they are moving from your catchment area!

The more you become aware of your reactions, the more control you will have. This leads us to the second key principle.

Behaviour is always a management issue

How can I get children to behave better?

Jill is a newly qualified teacher and is beginning to feel worn down by the constant interruptions to her lessons. All she seems to do is tell her children off. This seems to have short-lived impact on their behaviour.

Children's behaviour is affected by the way in which adults respond to them. Many children receive six negative responses to every positive one each day. It is not surprising therefore that many children are used to their behaviour obtaining negative attention from adults. Jill's task is to focus more on what her children are doing correctly, make a fuss of the positive. Effective teachers have a ratio of four positives for every one negative. It will take time for her children to change their behaviour, but it will work. This is what positive behaviour management is all about:

* Catch the children behaving well and praise/reward them.
* Shape their behaviour through small steps.
* Ignore inappropriate behaviour (when possible).

Over the last thirty years, the use of sanctions and punishment has been challenged as an effective way to help children learn how to behave appropriately. The problem is that there has not been enough emphasis on what exactly parents and teachers are supposed to do instead. Having removed the stick how can the carrot be used effectively? It was too often assumed that we did not need to be trained in new methods, they would just come naturally.

Try these classroom management techniques:

- develop routines for getting equipment, hands up for help, etc.
- start the lesson quickly with small tasks that lead to quick success
- use rewards for the whole class as well as individuals
- value effort as much as achievement
- manage by walkabout
- practise **the look**
- nip difficulties in the bud early, use non-verbal cues.

Behaviour always happens in a context

Why are they good sometimes, but not others?

Behaviour always happens somewhere with other people involved. A very good way to understand it is to carry out an ABC analysis:

- ⌘ A stands for antecedents — what happened before the problem behaviour you are concerned about (the triggers).
- ⌘ B is the behaviour.
- ⌘ C is the consequence — what happened after the behaviour.

If you can control either the A or C, you can change the behaviour.

Practise asking good questions. To understand any behaviour, develop a check list. This can save you a lot of time and help you to see more clearly what may be controlling the behaviour. Look for simple explanations for the behaviour. A child may have problems at home but this is not always the reason behind the behaviour. We should learn to control the controllable, not go in for theories of despair.

Some good questions:

- what exactly is the concern, describe what you can see?
- where does it usually happen?
- what happens before it?
- what happens after?
- who else is involved?
- does the child have learning difficulties?
- what are the usual consequences?
- have there been any changes at home?
- what have you tried already?
- does the child understand what is expected of them?
- do they have the necessary skills?
- what needs might the behaviour be meeting?
- when does the behaviour not happen?
- is the pupil unable, unwilling or unhappy?

Ask yourself: Why is this child behaving in this way at this time, in this place, with these people?

Behaviour always has a function

How can I know what lies behind the behaviour?

Children are usually trying to solve a problem not be one.

Carl always sits passively and will not start any set work until his teacher gives him a gentle nudge to get started.

Function —Nurture

Becky is quick to have an argument with any of her friends who stops her from having her own way.

Function — Control

John will often spoil other children's work if left unsupervised.

Function — Revenge

Sarah shouts out and is constantly asking, 'What do I do next?'

Function — Attention

Tim starts annoying his friends when new work is set.

Function — Escape

The behaviour we observe can be seen as a child's way of communicating with us. We can understand the 'why' of behaviour if we look to the consequences of the behaviour. When we think that we have a reasonable explanation, put some strategies in place to see if the behaviour begins to change. Below are some ideas for the different functions behaviour can have in school. Do not worry if you get it wrong — the same behaviour can serve several functions. For example: Simon frequently makes noises. This may be to:

- annoy his teacher
- to avoid work he finds difficult
- to impress his friends.

The only way of knowing why he does it is to look at the consequences and then put strategies in place that will enable the child to get his needs met in more appropriate ways.

For the child who needs nurture, try:

- ⌘ Highlighting their areas of competence.
- ⌘ Giving attention when the child takes the initiative.
- ⌘ Highlighting and using areas of knowledge/skill.
- ⌘ Giving clear roles in group work.
- ⌘ Sensitively supporting the child in friendships.

For the child who needs revenge, try:

- ⌘ Developing a self-esteem programme.
- ⌘ Establishing clear boundaries for acceptable behaviour.
- ⌘ Teaching the pupil to understand how other children feel.
- ⌘ Teaching self-control.
- ⌘ Letting the child practise other ways of expressing feelings.

For the child who needs control, try:

- ⌘ Giving the child responsibilities.
- ⌘ Getting the child used to carrying out small, reasonable requests.
- ⌘ When possible, giving choices.
- ⌘ Allowing the child to help others in an area of strength.
- ⌘ Asking for the child's help in improving matters.

For the child who needs to escape, try:

- ⌘ Rewarding effort as much as achievement.
- ⌘ Breaking tasks down into small manageable ones.
- ⌘ Reviewing progress, new skills learned.
- ⌘ Agreeing how the child can ask for your assistance.
- ⌘ Showing new skills that the child will achieve.

For the child who needs attention, try:

- ⌘ Rewarding appropriate behaviour with your attention.
- ⌘ Using a pay back system — tasks to be done in free time.
- ⌘ Sitting the child with a good role model.
- ⌘ Agreeing how often you will work with the child.
- ⌘ Rewarding short periods of success.

Key principles of positive behaviour management

⌘ Personal awareness increases personal control.
⌘ Behaviour is always a management issue — for everyone.
⌘ Behaviour always happens in a context.
⌘ Behaviour always has a function.

Dos and don'ts for improving behaviour

⌘ **Don't** try to change everything at once.
⌘ **Don't** wait until things get really bad before taking action.
⌘ **Don't** over-personalise issues.
⌘ **Do** develop a plan of action.
⌘ **Do** focus on small steps for improvement.
⌘ **Do** talk with colleagues.
⌘ **Do** have a life outside school.

Reference

Hill J, Maughan B, eds (2001) *Conduct disorders in childhood and adolescence*. Cambridge University Press, Cambridge

2

Empathy

The bridge across

There are many children who find it difficult to be kind and caring towards one another. They hit and push with little regard to the hurt and upset they may be causing others. Some people view such children as mean and spiteful. This is the way in which many people explain children's behaviour. As professionals we are forever emphasising that it is the act that should be condemned, not the child. This chapter will argue that when children feel that they are being personally blamed this can contribute towards a block in their ability to empathise with others which, in turn, increases the likelihood of their behaving aggressively and uncaringly towards their peers. This is because they feel ashamed of themselves, rather than guilty, which is a normal and manageable response. This can be summarised as follows:

> I did something wrong and I feel guilty. I am able to understand how others feel when they do something similar.
>
> I did something wrong. I feel ashamed of myself. I am less able to empathise with others.

Our aim is to help children behave in a pro-social way. Pro-social behaviour is voluntary behaviour that benefits another. Normally, pro-social behaviour develops through a child internalising the moral standards and beliefs of the community in which they grow up. Sadly, there will be some children who grow up in situations where they face many 'at risk' factors that work against them developing such pro-social behaviour.

At risk factors

If a child has or experiences 'at risk' factors, there is an increased likelihood that they will be negatively affected. It does not mean that because they have them they will have problems. Just as there are 'at risk' factors, there are also 'protective factors', which will ameliorate and greatly reduce the negative effects of the 'at risk' ones. (The concept of resiliency is relevant here.)

Home factors:

- aggressive role models at home
- inconsistent parenting
- early exposure to adult media
- drug/alcohol abuse by adults
- mentally ill carers
- neglect
- excessive pressure
- abuse — physical, sexual, emotional.

Community factors:

- poverty
- unemployment
- street delinquency

- drug culture.

While there are many negative factors that will affect a child's emerging empathy, there are low level, more fundamental aspects to this process. Some parents can resent the attention seeking behaviour of their infant. The parent might have an inappropriate idea of how independent children should be. This can contribute to a difficult relationship. A parent may find it difficult to hold enjoyable conversations with their child. Most interactions are directive. This can result in a child becoming rebellious and hostile towards the parent. This lack of social conversation means that a child's own verbal skills will suffer, along with their own social conversation skills. What this means is that the cognitive component of empathy, the ability to discern the feelings in others, especially another child's emotional responses to their behaviour, will be severely weakened.

One of the best antidotes to antisocial behaviour is a child's ability to empathise with others. We often focus on teaching children social skills when they lack this fundamental building block. If they are unable to empathise with others, they are unlikely to be motivated to behave appropriately. They are unable to imagine the negative effects their behaviour may be having on others.

Key terms and definitions

Empathy is the ability to have an emotional reaction similar to the one that we see another person experiencing. For example:

I feel sad because I see you crying.

Sympathy involves an understanding of what the other person is feeling based on knowledge of past experiences. For example:

I feel sorrow about your pet dying.

Guilt

When a child does something wrong, their attention is drawn to the negative consequences of their behaviour and the distress it may cause the person. Children are likely to feel guilty about their actions and to be motivated to learn to change. Guilt can then be constructive in helping children to develop positive relationships. Guilt is painful but is more associated with the person wanting to do something to undo the pain the act has caused. For example:

I did something horrible and I want to make amends.

Shame

Shame is a more devastating emotion and involves the person condemning themselves. A child who is told often that they are no good and worthless is likely to feel ashamed of him/herself. Shame acts as a block to children developing empathy. It is a more painful emotion leading to children feeling that they are worthless and powerless. Shame attacks the very personality, leading to the individual wanting to shrink away. For example:

I did something horrible, because I am horrible.

Is empathy innate or learned?

Imagine the situation. A six-month-old baby is lying awake in his/her pram. Nearby, an older child starts to cry. How will the baby react? Research, and everyday experience, tells us that the baby will start to cry as well. It seems that while the infant is not able yet to distinguish itself from another child, it is able to feel distress from their crying. This clearly suggests that the ability to feel another's pain is innate and not learned. As the child gets older he/she will learn to comfort another child who is in distress. He/she will take his/her own teddy bear to a distressed child in an attempt to comfort them. All of these examples highlight that empathy is an innate ability that children are born with. This ability may be suppressed through negative experiences, but it is fundamental to each of us.

Empathy and gender

Many people may think that boys are less empathic than girls. This is only partly true. It seems that both boys and girls are empathic, but that boys learn to be less empathic towards other boys that they do not know. It is OK for them to show empathy towards girls and boys that they know, but not towards boys they do not know. If this is the case, efforts to help boys understand and maintain their empathic skills will be an important contribution we can make towards them behaving pro-socially.

Measuring empathy

Below is a shortened questionnaire which aims to measure empathy in young children. You might like to try modifying some of the questions to see if the theory matches your findings.

The scoring is on a one to six scale, where six means applies exactly and one, does not apply.

The higher the score the more empathic the child is.

Applies exactly					Does not apply at all
1	2	3	4	5	6

Empathy questionnaire

1   When I see a girl who is hurt, I wish to help her.
2   It often makes me distressed when I see something sad on TV.
3   Seeing a boy who is sad makes me want to comfort him.
4   I feel very sorry for a student who is being bullied by others.
5   Sometimes I feel a bit distressed when I read or hear about something sad.
6   Seeing a girl who is sad makes me want to comfort her.
7   Seeing a girl who can't find anyone to be with makes me feel sorry for her.
8   When I see a boy who is distressed I sometimes feel like crying.
9   When I see a boy who is hurt, I wish to help him.
10   When I see a girl who is distressed I sometimes feel like crying.

11   Seeing a boy who can't find anyone to be with makes me feel sorry for him.

12   I want to help and comfort a student who is distressed.

As you can see questions 1, 6 and 7 have a girl as stimulus, while 3, 9, and 11 has a boy as stimulus. Questions 2, 5, 8 and 10 are measures of distress and 4 and 12 are general empathy questions. (This is adapted from a questionnaire devised by Olweus, 1989.)

Children who display behavioural problems often show a weakness in their ability to be empathic with others.

What can you do if you have a child that shows all the characteristics of not being empathic?

How to develop empathy

Each of us in our daily interactions with children use methods that are aimed to develop empathy. Because we do it so naturally we are often unaware of what we are doing. However, if we are trying to increase a child's ability to empathise, the more focused we are, the more effective the techniques we use are likely to be.

Below are some ideas — you may well be using some. Some might not be appropriate for the child you have in mind, just use the ones that are.

When talking with a child you can either use events that have happened, that they know about, or you could use stories or even TV programmes that you have both seen. The skill is to find a number of techniques that make sense to the child and to use these in a positive and caring manner. With each technique if you find that the child does not seem to have the necessary understanding then your task is to set up learning opportunities to help them. As with learning any skill, establish what they do know and, with your support, try to take them forward to a new level of understanding.

Inductive techniques

These techniques are based on helping children to look at specific events or specific rules and to work out from them to more general principles. It is a way of understanding unexperienced events through those events that are experienced. In so far as it is logically impossible for us too experience all events, all human knowledge is 'inductive knowledge'.

Justice

Does the child understand everyday rules that help us all to interact with each other in a safe and caring way. If they do, you can of course remind them of the rule that they have broken. What you are doing is highlighting an inconsistency that exists between what they believe and what they have done. Such psychological tensions can motivate change.

You upset Jane by pushing in front. Is that fair?

The next step is to help the child develop alternative ways to avoid the problem next time. This technique appeals to a child: moral sense of right and wrong.

Perspective

This approach will also enable you to develop some understanding as to the range of emotional terms the child has. You may well find that they are stumped for words. Try showing them a range of faces with different emotional expressions on them:

How do you think John felt when you took his toy?

If they have a limited range then this is clearly an area that you can help them to develop a wider range. Pictures and puppets might help.

Consequences

Through focusing on the affect of their behaviour you will gain insight into how the child explains events. Are they able to see that it is their behaviour that has caused another child pain and distress. Again, if not, it is worth telling them and showing them how things that we do affect others.

Look what you've done to Tom by taking his pencil. How would you feel if somebody took yours?

Rule violation

When a child has broken a rule that results in another child being hurt, establish whether or not they understand that they have broken a rule. Often they do not. Or, have selectively forgotten it for their own benefit. Work with them to learn core rules that relate to how they relate with other children:

Respect and care

What is the rule about sharing? What do you think would happen if nobody shared anything with anyone?

Reality based

Explore with the child a range of alternative behaviours :What do you think would happen if ... ? This will enable the child to see that by being more cooperative, their own needs could be better met as well as those of other children.

If you took turns you could both play the game.

Victim–orientated discipline

Emphasis is on apologies and reparation. With this technique the aim is to focus on the effect on the victim; their feelings and any other consequences. Sometimes it is possible to encourage a child to 'bin the sin'. That is, to do something to make up for the pain and upset that they have caused. This is pointless if there is no genuine empathy with the victim.

Preaching

This is perhaps the most commonly used technique. It is effective if the child's empathy/sympathy is engaged by highlighting benefits of altruism. The stronger a moral/religious code is in place, the more effective this is likely to be.

Modelling

Significant adults model appropriate behaviour. Most children will have heroes, in the family, sport, media or adults in school. Highlighting how they would behave in a range of situations can encourage children to behave similarly.

Reinforcement

Praise that explains the child's behaviour as being part of their personal disposition or motivation will be more effective::

You helped John with his work because you are a kind person.

It is important to help children develop positive attributes by which they can explain their own behaviour.

Empathy can be developed in young children either through group activities delivered through assemblies, circle time, or, on a one-to-one basis. Many children who face emotional and behavioural barriers can lack this basic, but essential skill. Through increasing our understanding we can develop support plans which include techniques that we know can help children to understand what it is like to stand in someone else's shoes.

Reference

Bohart A, Stipek D (2001) *Constructive and Destructive Behaviour*. American Psychological Association

Strayhorn J (1988) *The Competent Child*. The Guilford Press, New York

3

Listening to children

Listening to children has always been important, but recent world-wide events serve to remind us that children today often receive traumatic information of which they then have to make sense. It is both frustrating and disheartening to sit with a child who is clearly unhappy, but unable to talk with us. We may have ideas about how we may help but these are to no purpose if there is a lack of communication. By becoming aware of basic counselling and listening skills applicable to children, it is possible to start overcoming the communication barriers and develop a useful rapport.

To help children we must help them teach us about themselves

Children nowadays face many challenges, conflicts and pressures. As adults we value childhood and seek to protect children through making their rights explicit.

These rights include:

- being allowed to learn
- the right to care and safety
- the right to be listened to
- the right to be consulted

- the right to be different
- the right to be valued
- the right to have fun.

While most adults support these ideals they can find it difficult to respond to children as they would like. There is a 'culture gap' between us and children. This can add to the difficulties experienced by children. Unless we can understand the world in which children are growing up we will be less able to support them through the challenges they face. These can range from coping with learning difficulties to the trauma of parents separating and divorce.

We cannot know what it is like to be a child today, which is why we need them to teach us — only then can we offer support. We need to learn to listen in order to learn.

Active listening

The aim of listening to children is to enable the youngster to feel heard and understood. So often children are 'told' what they should or should not do, think or feel. They learn not to speak about themselves — the adults in their lives having more than enough to say!

We need to encourage children to do most of the talking as they are the experts on their situation. Our aim **must** be to get them to **teach** us about themselves.

We need to promote the following skills in order to listen; paraphrasing, reflecting feelings, summarising, and focusing.

These will help you develop empathy and show your unconditional acceptance of the child.

Think carefully of the questions you are asking — they may not be the right questions. Are they more like an interrogation with the child only answering 'yes' or 'no'?

To listen supportively, we need to ask 'open ended' questions. For example, 'Tell me how you felt?' rather than 'Were you upset?'

Remember, a key aim is to explore the feelings that a child has experienced, promoting understanding which leads to effective action. This may be done through direct questioning or through the use of activities such as drawing, play, make-believe, clay modeling — any medium which allows the child to get in touch with feelings. This is important, as it is only when the feelings are faced that they can learn to cope with them. While listening, look for themes or patterns in what the child is or is not telling you. Note how the story is being told and the dominant feelings expressed to you.

For example, a child who has experienced rejection will often feel angry but may not feel safe to express this emotion for fear of further rejection. The emotion may well be expressed indirectly, possibly through aggression or bullying. To enable these feelings to be resolved the child needs to be supported in facing the anger and becoming aware of this as a normal, acceptable response. Children will often need reassurance that the feelings they are experiencing are normal and not a sign that they are abnormal in some way.

There are times when we will wish to help children understand what they are feeling. When Daryl Peek was faced with just such a challenge in her school she used a bottle of pop to help her children understand that bad events can shake us, just like a fizzy drink. Our emotions are like the fizz inside which needs to come out in a way that is safe both for us and others.

Such a simple but clear explanation can help children to make sense of what they may be feeling, and it can be reassuring to see that an adult understands.

Listening style

The listener's attitude towards the child needs to be one of trust and acceptance — a child will sense if someone can be trusted or not. The listener must not judge the child but accept him or her unconditionally. The non-verbal manner of the listener needs to be relaxed with a gentle, unhurried voice.

Remember the aim is to :

- convey non-judgmental acceptance of the child
- enable the child to talk freely and openly
- discuss worries and difficulties that are important and sensitive
- help the child gain awareness and understanding
- enable the child to take control of those aspects of his/her life as far as is possible.

To help to achieve this the listener must:

- be aware of eye contact — excessive eye contact can be threatening and uncomfortable while too little can be interpreted as boredom or disinterest
- use verbal and non-verbal encouragers, eg. head nods, 'I see', etc
- understand and use silence
- show genuine interest

- actively aim to understand the child's concerns
- express empathy
- help the child to focus on the central aspect of the concern, if there is one
- listen for the feelings — the music behind the words
- listen for the possible cause of the concern — to develop insight with the child
- help the child establish a link between the problem and possible causes
- develop an understanding of the child's role in the problem and help develop the child's problem solving skills.

Don't:

- argue
- interrupt
- give unasked-for advice
- jump to conclusions
- psychologise
- over-react
- belittle their difficulties
- finish suddenly.

Some phrases to avoid:

> *I know how you feel.*
> *Don't worry, it will be OK.*
> *If I were you I'd......* (give information, not advice)

When listening and talking to young children:

- use short sentences — no more than three to five words longer than the child's sentence
- use the child's words
- use names rather than pronouns
- do not ask the child, 'Do you understand?' Ask them to repeat your message
- rephrase questions that the child does not understand
- do not respond to every answer with another question — a short summary will encourage the child to expand on the previous statement.

The importance of silence

Most of us find silence difficult to manage, trying to fill the gap in conversation at all costs.

However, silence can be a positive experience in which the child has the right to determine the nature and pace of the interview, and the listener, through his skills, can use it as another tool to enable communication.

In order to use silence effectively, the listener needs to accept its worth, to feel confident about allowing it to continue and be sensitive as to why it is happening.

Interpreting silence

Silence can express many emotions and the listener should make every attempt to understand the reason behind the silence by observing the child's movements, gestures, tone of voice and physical appearance. Commenting on these observations can result in the child agreeing with you or correcting your observation. Either way, the child has been engaged in conversation in a constructive manner.

Different kinds of silence can include:

⌘ The silence of thought — the child may be reflecting on the situation and sorting out his thoughts. If this endures, the listener may wish to help with, 'There must be lots to think of, are you ready to tell me some of it?'

⌘ The silence of trauma — when something shocking or frightening has been raised and time is needed to absorb it.

⌘ The silence of confusion — the child may not understand what is being said or asked. Rephrasing may help.

⌘ The silence of uncertainty — the child may not know/understand what is expected. He may need information as to how to proceed, eg. 'It must be difficult to get started, it may help by telling me what you felt when...'

⌘ The silence of resistance — often the most difficult to bear as it easy for the listener to feel rejected or challenged. Try not to take this personally — you may be viewed as an authority figure or the child may not be ready to tell you what is troubling him. See the situation from the child's point of view, 'I don't mind the silence, but I feel you are not happy with me in some way. It may help if you tell me about it'.

⌘ The silence of protection — a form of shield against adult intrusions. The child may have tried to share his difficulties and pain only to have them rebuffed, undervalued or dismissed. Support and reassurance is needed to regain a sense of trust.

⌘ The silence of preparation — the child is thinking or
   rehearsing what to say. The listener may rush in to fill the
   silence and interrupt these thoughts.
⌘ The silence of the listener — explain your own silences,
   'I'm just thinking about what you said'.

Goals of listening

Through active listening you can enable children to talk about
their feelings and experiences. The task of listening supportively
is to enable children to become aware of their feelings and the
consequences for themselves and others of their behaviour. If
they lack a 'feeling vocabulary' you may employ a range of
'smiley faces' with different expressions.

When listening remember to keep checking. 'Do you
understand what is being said?' If the answer is no, be prepared
to ask for further information/clarification.

Your role as listener is to help children work through their
difficulties/concerns, to understand feelings and to consider
options to improve matters. Not only will you be helping the
situation now, but you will also be teaching the child a problem-
solving approach for the future.

Working with parents

A common area of difficulty can be when we meet with
parents/carers to discuss concerns about some aspect of a child's
behaviour. Sadly, because of past personal experiences some
adults approach school with negative and hostile feelings. It is
hard for us to appreciate that the place we work in each day can

be so negatively experienced (a bit like hospitals). A meeting intended to help and support a child can so easily degenerate into an argument with both sides taking up entrenched positions.

When holding meetings avoid:

- too many professionals being present
- jargon
- presenting reports that have not been seen by home first.

We each have the skills needed to work with parents but in various degrees. We are often so unconsciously skilled that we are not even aware of possessing them. However, for most of us there are times when we get it wrong, and we are well aware of it. Some of the core skills are outlined below. We can always improve a skill through awareness and practise.

Receiving negative feedback

If a parent has some valid criticism about what has happened in school, acknowledge the validity. If you are unsure about its validity decide the additional information you will need before making a decision. If there is an element of personal put down, do not accept the put down. Stay with the behaviour. For example, letters were not sent home because you never keep any promises, 'Let's stay with the facts, I'll accept that we did not send letters home.'

Giving negative feedback

Try to acknowledge positive improvements and changes before making a negative point. Make sure that you are being specific and clear, give an example. Emphasise that it is the behaviour that you are concerned about, the individual child is fine. Ask for their ideas as to how improvements may be achieved. Avoid being the expert, they know more about the child in question than you ever will.

Communication as muscle power

Avoid giving ambiguous messages. For example, don't say 'will you ....' when it is something they have to do. 'I would like it if you', is softer than, 'It is important that you', which is softer than, 'It is essential that you', which is softer than, 'I demand that you'.

Being assertive

If you are going to hold a difficult meeting it will help if you make some notes beforehand. What do you need to achieve for the meeting to be successful.

What compromises are you prepared to make.

> **R** emember, Even Fish need confidence
> **E** Describe the Event that you need to talk about
> **F** What are the Feelings you have to do with this event
> **N** What do you Need to happen
> **C** What will be the Consequences if these changes do not occur

Value and respect

Take time to listen to the other person's point of view. Ask them what they have tried. Why do they think it worked/didn't work? Ask them to describe times when the behaviour is good, or marginally better. Why do they think this is so. Try to build on their suggestions and ideas. Acknowledge that they are probably going through a difficult time.

Being genuinely listened to is one of the most powerful inter-personal tools that exists. To experience someone make an effort to understand our view point is a rare experience. We are all so busy that half the time we hear what we think other people have said rather than what they actually have said. Through listening we not only build a bridge to the other person, child or adult, but we also increase their own sense of value and competency.

References

Long R (2002) *Facing Lions*. Education Works, 4 Glendale Terrace, Castle Hill, Totnes, Devon TQ9 5NY

Peek D (2002) *Dealing With Trauma*. Spellbinder Education, 42 West Street, Harrietsham, Kent ME17 1HU

4

Understanding loss

We have come a long way in understanding how children react and cope with loss. In the past, we often over-protected children from sad events because we thought it was 'best for them' if they did not face the harsh realities of life until they were older. We would avoid taking children to funerals because of the upset it would cause. But, today, we appreciate much more the need for children to express their grief like adults and to have a sense of a final goodbye. Today, we appreciate the need to be open and support children when they face losses. I can well remember when I first became involved in grief counselling for children. The father in me would wish to avoid talking to a young boy or girl of the loss of a mum or dad, because of the obvious pain it would cause them. It took time and confidence to realise that tears can be healing.

I was equally worried about saying the wrong thing, of making matters worse. But I now remember something a friend once told me. She told how her first husband died and how people she knew would cross the road to avoid saying the wrong thing. She later married again and moved to a Mediterranean country, where sadly her second husband died. She noticed how people there would cross the road to offer her comfort. Even though they often said the wrong thing, they made the right choice.

Little deaths

Too often when we think of loss we think about the big ones. The tragic death of parents, grandparents or siblings. But the truth is that children of all ages face numerous 'little losses' throughout their lives. Some examples are:

- death of a pet
- friends moving away
- changing teachers
- changing schools
- favourite toys.

Loss pervades our lives. As an adolescent son or daughter leaves the house every mum and dad has to accept the loss of their own adolescence. Those who work with children with special educational needs can forget that these children can also struggle with emotions that reflect their own loss. The dyslexic pupil who struggles to do what their peers seem to do effortlessly experiences loss. The physically disabled child has the loss of their own mobility that they see others possess.

Attachment

Any loss means that some form of attachment has been broken. We are all biologically programmed to attach to our carers. It makes good biological sense. Without close, attentitive care, children can not survive. When such bonds are broken the pain that results is a natural healthy pain. Children cannot love or be attached to people and objects they value and not feel any hurt when they lose them. It would be psychologically inconsistent not to have an emotional reaction in such circumstances. We can observe loss reactions in very young children. Babies cry when their mum or dad leaves the room. Their crying is an angry, 'You come back here' cry. They are protesting. Equally, we invest emotional attachment into objects and places as well as people.

Reactions to loss

Have you noticed how different children will react differently when separated from their carers? Some children will cry and protest for a long time, others will withdraw and become depressed and passive. When 'mum' returns, some will be angry with her and almost seem to punish her for 'abandoning them'. Some will become clingy and not let her out of their sight. Such reactions highlight again how complex behaviour is. It is determined by many interlocking factors. In this case, the child's own temperament is playing a central role in determining how the child will react.

Loss determinants

There are many factors which determine how children respond to loss. These are:

- nature of the attachment
- child's temperament/personality
- social factors
- previous losses
- cause of the loss.

The last point is, of course, important. While there are similarities between loss that is the result of death and loss through family breakdown, there are many differences. When a family finally breaks down and parents/carers separate this is a public event that officially marks the end of a relationship. But the effect to children may have been taking place before. Divorce is best seen as a process rather than a single event. It is what happens prior to the divorce that is more significant to children in the family. The possible loss of love, care, etc may effect a child's in-school behaviour long before the adults decide to separate. Children may experience uncertainty, self-blame, anger and despair. Equally, it should be emphasised that for many children family separation can enable them to grow in love and security within a single parent family. Although, at the time, many children may prefer an unhappy family life rather than a separated one, in the long run the benefits can outweigh any misconstrued advantages.

Reactions to loss include:

- bedwetting, (regression)
- aggressive behaviour
- eating/sleeping disorders
- headaches, tummy upsets — psychosomatic disorders
- learning difficulties
- withdrawal
- dependency
- irritability
- separation difficulties, clinginess
- anxiety

Children coping with loss in school may withdraw from learning and lack motivation. In fact, any disturbance in a child's usual behaviour can be a reaction to loss.

Cultural myths

If a child of four came into the room and found an adult crying they would probably give them a hug. They might even start crying with them. Very young children are more closely in touch with their feelings and display them more honestly and fully. As children learn about their social world they begin to adopt the cultural myths that their group has towards feelings.

Some of the most powerful ones are:

- be strong — don't cry
- cry alone — not in public
- keep busy — distract yourself
- time will heal
- cheer up.

These myths can mean that strong emotions are bottled up within the child. Usually, when a loved one dies, or moves away, the family are left with a mixture of emotions. Many of these are strong feelings of sadness and regret. But there are often more negative ones: anger and guilt. Because it is not so acceptable to express these, children will hold them in.

Children do not feel that it is right to express such negative emotions so they try to hold them in. But, such emotions seek some form of expression. Imagine a kettle beginning to boil.

The pressure of steam will find some way out, even if the lid is firmly being held in place.

Acting out

A child experiencing loss will find some way in which the emotional pressure within can be released. They might not feel safe to do this at home. School is often the place where they will act out such negative emotions. Being aggressive towards peers, cheeky to adults can be a child's way of telling the world about their anger for being abandoned.

> Guiding principles:
> ❖ emotional reactions to loss are normal
> ❖ children can be happy in one setting, not in another
> ❖ loss can involve many emotions, sadness, anger, guilt

The skilled helper aims to help the child to:

- accept the loss, 'I wish it hadn't happened, but it has'
- express their feelings
- accept their feelings as normal.

This is achieved by:

- being open, honest and accepting

- listening to good and bad memories in a non-judgemental way
- being there when needed
- accepting questions to which they don't have answers
- giving them time.

Core aims

Within school it is not our place as school staff to pretend that we are 'grief counsellors'. But we can offer more sensitive and valuable support if we hold some key aims in our mind. Whenever a relationship ends, whether it is through bereavement, family break up or friends falling out, these aims will hold true.

Say sorry for things said that shouldn't have been

Children will often remember thoughts that were said or unsaid, that were harmful and hurtful towards a person. When these are acknowledged in spoken or written form they can have their sting removed.

Forgive things done that hurt the child

A child may well feel aggrieved at something the adult or friend said or did that hurt them. It can assuage the pain through a child acknowledging that they have been hurt and forgiving the person.

Acknowledge feelings: how the child felt

There are always strong and positive emotional attachments that are not said often enough. A child can benefit through consciously recognising and either telling or writing these feelings down.

Happy memories

Loss can often overwhelm those other strong and happy feelings. Helping a child to remember such times using, for example, photographs can ensure that they come to appreciate that the pain they felt at the loss of their loved one reflected the strength of love they held towards them.

Ultimately, we each learn to cope with loss. Too often negatively bottled-up emotions detract from an appreciation of the positive emotions that also exist. Neither is right nor wrong. We have emotions that reflect the feelings of having, of being with others. Children see themselves in the eyes of those who care for them. But, just as there are positive emotions for having, there are also emotions of losing.

When Children Grieve tells of a young boy whose hamster has died (James and Friedman, 2001). His mother contacted them to ask how she could help the little boy cope with this loss. The counsellors explained that given his age, he probably would not need any help. He was too young to have been influenced by those cultural myths. The mother overheard her little boy talking to his hamster. This is what he said:

> *Mr Hamster, you were a good hamster. I'm sorry for the*
> *times I did not clean your cage. I was mad the time you*

*bit me, but that's OK. I wish you didn't have to get sick
and die. I wanted to play with you more. I loved you,
and I know you loved me. Goodbye Mr Hamster.*

When the cousellors heard this, they recorded it. This little boy
had encapsulated in his young mind the entire therapeutic
approach of the counsellors. He had:

- said sorry to the hamster
- forgiven the hamster
- acknowledged his feelings
- remembered happy times.

The approach endorsed by these experienced counsellors
involves helping children review the relationship. It is unspoken
and unexpressed feelings that will lead children to acting out, or
acting in through withdrawal, depression and anxiety, as a way
of relieving and coping with the internal emotional tensions they
are experiencing.

General support

- Help them express their feelings.
- Give permission to feel the way they do, cry, be angry, etc.
- Use stories, music, poetry.
- Clarify any distortions and misperceptions, 'I understand
  how you feel... but that is not what really happened.'
- Involve special friends.
- Provide clear and simple information.
- Be mindful of special days, mothers'/fathers' day

Children coping with loss may quickly form a strong attachment with a substitute adult.

The more loss is included and talked about, the more we can enable children to make sense of the overwhelming emotions that loss can cause. To a young child, the pain can be frightening when no one has told you that such reactions are normal.

Don't:
- Say I know how you feel
- Say you must be brave for Mummy
- Give answers to the unanswerable
- Push them to 'talk about it'
- Answer questions they haven't asked

Do:
- Be available
- Provide bolt holes
- Listen, be patient
- Help them find peers who can be supportive
- Accept how they feel
- Keep them busy, involved in daily routines

Do I need to be a counsellor?

Schools are where children bring and express their feelings of loss. School staff do not have to be trained therapists or cousellors to give support that can make a difference to a child who is coping with whatever kind of loss. Naturally, the more informed and trained we are, the more confident we will be in supporting children. While there are many useful insights and techniques that counselling can offer us, we have always to just reach out to listen and offer comfort to each other. This is because we are able to empathise with another's distress.

Loss in the classroom

Many children are 'labelled' as having special needs. Perhaps they need additional support to master reading skills that their peers learn very quickly. Loss is something that many children have to learn to cope with because they cannot manage the size of the 'learning step' with which they are faced. As a result, these children will often experience a sense of loss — a loss of being unable to do what their peers do. Perhaps they have physical differences or limitations. Again, we need to understand that many children struggle with a negative sense of identity. They can develop a sense of sadness because they feel and believe that they are not like other children. Such children need both understanding and support, as well as advocates who will challenge the system on their behalf.

In the past, loss was seen as a negative emotional experience, similar to hitting your finger with a hammer. It took time to heal, the assumption was that 'time heals all wounds'. Today, we understand better that the pain children experience depends on a number of factors. These include the child's emerging personality, combined with their coping strategies and other life experiences.

The better we can support children and help make school as positive an experience as possible.

Reference

James J, Friedman R (2001) *When Children Greive*. Harper Collins, New York

5

Playground survival skills

Let's be honest — the one time of the day that nearly all children enjoy is 'playtime'. This is when children interact with their peers on their own terms, with minimum supervision. It is when they can develop friendship skills, ball game skills as well as many other essential skills. They learn their position in the group and see how emotions are expressed and conflicts resolved. It is also a rare time for any child when adult supervision is at a minimum. For some children, the fact that there are fewer adults around can cause anxiety. The playground is where bullying is most likely to occur.

Young children in a play group are not too bothered about who they sit with or who is with them in the playground. This is that age where we observe parallel play. Children playing alongside each other but not interacting with each other. Gradually though, social interactive play emerges. Gender identification means that there are some activities more preferred by boys and some by girls. The reasons for such differences are probably the result of both biological and social factors. Five and six-year-old children are concerned about who they are playing with and the activities that they are doing. They may tell tales on each other, but their lack of skills means that minor disputes can be readily resolved with a few gentle questions, 'What were you doing?' and some simple solutions, 'Why don't you bring your own skipping rope in tomorrow'.

Free-time is important for any child's development. Play at school allows children to relax from the ever growing pressures that they face in class. Sadly, for an increasing number of children, playtime can cause more problems than it solves. For such children being in an interesting, well-structured lesson is preferable to the 'free for all' outside. It is not uncommon for schools to shorten lunchtimes because of the number of problems that occur at this time. The attitude is often one of, 'get them in, get them working and get them out'.

If we are to support children who experience interaction difficulties during playtime, we need to develop an understanding at two levels:

⌘ Is it a skill issue? Are they unable, unwilling or unhappy to play with their peers?
⌘ Is it a group issue? Do their difficulties stem from their being unable to work as a positive group member?

Without such an understanding we are likely to jump to conclusions as to the nature of the difficulties and put in place interventions that are not based on a real understanding of the issues involved. The most important thing for any practitioner working with children is to have a good theory. Once we have an understanding, the interventions will follow quite readily. Without such an understanding, we are acting in the dark.

A commonsense understanding

> Is the child:
> ❖ unable?
> ❖ unhappy?
> ❖ unwilling?

Unable — a skill deficit

Does the child have the necessary skills?

> Tom seems unable to share any toys with other children. He seems to enjoy being with other children and seeks them out to play but fails to play appropriately.

Reasons

There are rarely simplistic explanations for complicated behaviours. It is worth noting that schools today require a different set of skills from ten or so years ago. In the past, children were expected to be 'seen and not heard'. This approach was true for both home and school. In school, traditional learning methods meant that children sat in rows and listened to the teacher. This kind of learning is generally passive. Children come into school empty and school fills them up with knowledge. Today, we expect children to be active learners; that is, they contribute their ideas, share with others and give critical feedback. Skills such as turn taking, team playing, and compromise are skills that many children have not learnt outside of school.

Interventions

To support children in acquiring these skills imagine that your task is to 'scaffold' them from where they are to where you want them to be. Find out what they can do on their own and what they can do with some support. Just as we break learning down into small manageable steps, we need to do the same with behavioural skills:

⌘ Explain the reason for the skill.
⌘ Show them examples of the skill.
⌘ Let them practice the skill — with support
⌘ Let them practice the skill on their own.
⌘ Give them positive feedback.

Unhappy — performance deficit

Does the child have the skill but fail to use it appropriately for emotional reasons?

> When playing with one or two other children, Sarah behaves really well, but when the group is bigger she withdraws and plays on her own.

Reasons

Many children can behave well on a one-to-one basis or when in small groups, but once they are faced with many other peers their behaviour quickly deteriorates. The issue here may be to do with their need to 'belong'. This is a powerful need that we all have. In such situations, children can feel their position within the group is under threat. While some children will engage with other children aggressively to protect their position, others will withdraw. It is as if they fear the failure of trying to belong to the group but failing. Such children may have missed out on early experiences to socialise with other children. Each of us in competitive conditions have a range of options:

- fight
- give in
- compromise
- withdraw.

Sarah seems to be a child who copes with challenging situations by withdrawing.

Interventions

- Build self-esteem.
- Involve Sarah in group activities that she knows well.
- Increase group size slowly.
- Use a buddy system to help include her more.

Unwilling — self-control deficit

Does the child lose the ability to control his/her behaviour appropriately and acts in a defiant and confrontational manner?

> John plays well with other children when he is able to control what is going on. If another child tries to assert themself he very quickly becomes frustrated and will push other children aggressively.

Reasons

How children who wish to dominate others and be the 'leader' of a group cope with challenges is determined by many factors. If they have an aggressive disposition and have seen aggression used as a 'tool' to solve problems, they are more likely to resort to aggressive behaviour when frustrated in obtaining a goal they desire. If a child also has a low tolerance of frustration then the likelihood of aggressive outbursts will be significantly increased.

Interventions

⌘ Teach John relaxation techniques: breathe deeply, count to ten.
⌘ Praise him when he manages to keep calm.
⌘ Use sanctions that teach John to learn new skills (loss of free-time)
⌘ Frequently ask him to carry out reasonable requests, and praise him for helping.

Often interventions in one of these areas will suffice. However, there will be some children who do not respond to these interventions. At such times an alternative approach is as follows.

Making sense of groups

Happy, well-adjusted children function well in groups. The roles that they take up will include team leader, sharer, friend, listener, helper, etc. However, some children come to school with a range of basic unmet needs. They may not feel that they belong, or that they have enough control in their lives. Perhaps they have become extremely dependent on others, or perhaps they have poor co-ordination skills because of medical factors. Such unfilled needs motivate them to take up roles that seem to get their needs met but in a less than appropriate way. They are likely to fill such roles as bully, loner, comedian, pet, attention seeker, etc.

When children are in groups there are three key factors that will shape their behaviour:

1 The influence that they have within the group — how much control they have or need to have.
2 The degree of belonging to the group — the importance of having friends, of being popular.
3 The extent to which they can help the group achieve its goals — team games, ball games, pretend play, etc.

Difficulties in each of these areas results in children taking up less positive roles. While each of these factors interact with each other it is useful to consider them separately.

The need for control

This is a normal need, but some children will try to exert excessive influence on a group. They often fail to appreciate how their dominating behaviour negatively affects their peers. There may be many reasons for this, but the original cause of a behaviour does not need to be known to do something about it. All behaviour is determined by a range of factors — genetics, family, individual temperament, emotional, social, cognitive factors and others. It is rare to be able to say quite simply what caused any specific behaviour. (When people think that they can they are simplifying something that is very complicated. For example, is there a simple explanation as to why you are reading this book?) Children who have a strong need for control can be in danger of becoming, at best, bossy and, at worst, a bully.

Indicative questions

Does the child:

⌘ Display aggressive behaviour to obtain his/her own way?
⌘ Show little concern at other children's distress?
⌘ Fail to accept how his/her behaviour hurts others?

Interventions

⌘ Teach a vocabulary of feelings.
⌘ Help them to choose ways to express feelings and self-control techniques.
⌘ Develop empathy skills, eg. 'How would you feel if ...?'
⌘ Build their self-esteem.

⌘ Win-win outcomes — where nobody loses.

The need to belong

We all need to feel that we belong, it is a basic human need. But for many reasons, some children can become passive in group situations which may result in their becoming isolated and lonely. Such children can often have their passive and withdrawn behaviour reinforced by those well-meaning adults who will give them attention all the more.

Indicative questions

Does the child:

⌘ Rarely spontaneously join in group games?
⌘ Show signs of anxiety in social situations?
⌘ Prefer to remain close to adults?

Interventions

⌘ Build self-esteem.
⌘ Friendship skills, sharing, turn taking, etc.
⌘ Communication skills.
⌘ Team games.

Group goal

For children to work successfully as a group member it is helpful if they can contribute to the group goal. In class, this will often be learning goals set by the teacher. In such circumstances a child who faces learning difficulties can struggle to 'save face' in front of others. It is not uncommon to hide his/her difficulties from peers by becoming disruptive or passive. Note that it is not uncommon for girls to talk through their difficulties whereas boys often mask theirs with problem behaviour. Such problem behaviour results in getting them into more trouble and further behind in their work. During free-time, such skills that can help children support the group goals will be ball skills, group games, knowledge of music and fashion, for example.

Indicative questions

Does the child:

⌘ Show poor co-ordination skills?
⌘ Fail to understand and follow the rules of the game?

Interventions

⌘ Teach co-ordination skills.
⌘ Rehearse rules of games with children.
⌘ Use games involving one or two peers.

The next time a pupil in your class is having difficulties in the playground, try the following steps:

Step 1: Describe the problem as clearly and fully as you can. Always discuss your concerns with the child's parents.
Step 2: Observe how often it happens, where and who else is involved? What was happening before the behaviour and what followed it? You should always obtain

some base line data. Without this data you will not be able to see the very small signs of improvement.

Step 3: Analyse and hypothesise what appears to be a reasonable explanation for the behaviour?

Step 4: Interventions — decide which strategies you are going to use.

Step 5: Observe — collect new data and compare with previous data.

Step 6: Review — Is there any change in the behaviour? If not, repeat this process. If yes, give yourself a big well done sticker, and go home early!

Core skills

You may wish to consider the following areas that relate to the playground. If these areas are proactively addressed then many disputes and problems that children experience in the playground can be avoided.

Children learn core play skills through observation and experience. For those who struggle we can act proactively and set up systems and procedures that help identify such children increasing their awareness, understanding and skills.

> ❖ Problem-solving skills help children face the many challenges they face with tools to tackle everyday difficulties.
> ❖ Leadership skills can help those children who may over-dominate others as well as those who tend to be excessively passive in group situations.

Arguments occur naturally within any relationship. The key skill is learning how to 'fight fairly'.

Joining in is a central aspect of the playground. Approaching others with a view to joining in with them can be an incredibly difficult task for many children.

Communication is at the heart of any relationship and is a skill that many children with emotional and behavioural difficulties struggle with more than most. Training in specific skills can enable many children to avoid a wide range of pitfalls.

Games require a range of skills, fine and gross motor skills. All children will benefit from additional training and practice in this area, and for some children it will make a huge difference.

6

The resilient child

The expectation is that children who experience traumas in the early years will be severely affected later in life. For some this is true, but for a significant number their lives reflect an affirmation for life, a sense of stubborn durability and a compassion for others. Not exactly what you might expect. It seems that many children are steeled by adversity, not weakened.

We are so concerned with the difficulties and problems that children face that we pay little attention to understanding what it is that enables them to cope with adversity. For example, many children experience the divorce of their parents, but for the most part they cope successfully.

We seem to know more about risk factors in children's lives than what provides protection. It is right that we support those who have been hurt or traumatised, but it is equally important that we teach children essential life skills. Life is not problem free. Most of the time we cope successfully with the challenges we meet, although we do not always appreciate this fact. We only see something as a challenge when we fail to cope effectively with it. We are often so problem-orientated that we pay little attention to how we might be able to avoid problems in the first place. Early preventative work is an essential feature to all those whose key aim is to enrich the lives of the children with whom they work.

The marshmallow test

Imagine you are four years old. You are sitting in front of a marshmallow and told that you can either eat it immediately or wait until the adult returns and have two. What would you do? Would you be impulsive and eat it or would you distract yourself to have two later?

This was an experiment carried out by Walter Mischel and Philip Peake in 1990 and reported by Daniel Goleman (1996). They followed the children in their experiment onto their secondary schools and found that those who were impulsive tended to have more relationship difficulties. It seems that being impulsive can be a strong trait in some children. If we could teach children how to understand, express and control their emotions we would be giving them skills that would help them avoid many problems. This is what developing resiliency is all about.

In the past we could rely on kith and kin to teach children those life skills that are essential to adapting successfully to life's challenges. More and more today, we need to develop formal systems to achieve this end. Schools are ideally placed to achieve this and are growing in confidence in carrying out this role.

Resiliency is the term used to describe a child's ability to cope successfully, despite challenging and threatening circumstances. Such circumstances could include:

- bereavement
- parental separation
- illness
- conflicts.

Competency refers to those skills that are employed in ways appropriate to particular circumstances. It enables children to limit the damage done to them by negative events. Our challenge is to promote the skills which increase their resiliency.

Together, these concepts can offer a framework to work positively with young children to enhance their ability to adapt and cope. The earlier we teach and encourage competency skills the more resilient they can become. Some of the everyday challenges that children face will include:

- sibling rivalry
- separation from friends
- loss of loved objects.

There are many situations that provoke emotions such as fear, anxiety, sadness and anger in young children. A child's existing skills and emotional support that he/she is receiving from adults will determine whether or not he/she copes successfully under such circumstances. In school we have limited control over what happens to a child outside school, but we can try to make our support in school as purposeful as possible.

Children are trying to solve problems, not to be a problem, but without the right skills they are likely to develop less than appropriate solutions. It is not uncommon for their solutions to draw them to our attention. Their solutions become concern for us. Two examples are as follows:

> Sally is so used to being the centre of attention at home that in school she over-dominates her friends. This leads to her being left out of games because the other children become resentful or frightened of her.

Sally is attempting to meet her needs but because of her weakness in social skills is creating an even bigger problem for herself.

> Ben has a sensitive temperament and can easily feel anxious and overwhelmed in new situations. His solution to this problem is to avoid new situations. His tearfulness at such times naturally results in him being cuddled and comforted, which is reinforcing his avoidance of new situations.

Ben is meeting his need for security by avoiding new situations, but this is leading to him becoming socially isolated and falling behind in his work.

To develop resiliency we need to be clear as to which skills we wish to teach children. We will then need a range of techniques to help us teach these skills appropriately.

There are two things we need to do to achieve an increase in the resiliency and competency of the children we teach.

Decide essential skills to be achieved

Relationships

We all live our lives through relationships, but rarely are we taught the skills that can help us succeed in them. Having positive relationships has been found to be one of the best antidotes to a wide range of mental illnesses. It is relationships that often cause children distress and relationships that give the greatest joy.

Key skills
- ❖ listening
- ❖ joining in
- ❖ sharing
- ❖ turn taking
- ❖ respect

Confidence

Being confident is the key to children being able to risk learning. Without a positive sense of self they can be trapped in their own sense of inferiority instead of competence. Confidence is the oxygen that enables them to succeed in learning. If you have little, you risk little.

Key skills
- ❖ positive thinking
- ❖ humour
- ❖ target setting
- ❖ relaxation
- ❖ exercise

Control

This relates to confidence, in that having some control over your world gives a child a sense of mastery, a 'me do it' attitude. The less control children have, the less they feel able to affect change in their lives. A passive attitude can develop.

Key skills
* responsibilities
* choice
* self-control
* beliefs
* will-power

Emotion

Children learn from home how to express a wide range of emotions. In school there is a need to understand and to be able to control these emotions. Feeling angry is acceptable but hitting someone is not.

Key skills
* knowing feelings
* causes of feelings
* expressing feelings
* controlling feelings
* empathy

Decide the techniques to use

Knowing the skills we wish children to learn leads us to the question, 'How do we teach them these skills?' Children can learn the above skills in a wide range of different ways. The following factors will determine which aspect of the skill is to be developed.

⌘ Level of understanding (cognitive).
⌘ Existing skills (behaviour).
⌘ Emotional development (affective).

Ideally we want children to be competent in what they **feel** (affective), **do** (behaviour) and **know** (cognitive). We now need a range of techniques that can be used to help children learn the essential skills.

Techniques

Affective

Empathy: Use stories to help the child imagine that he/she is in the shoes of the other person, 'What would they be feeling?'

Awareness: Use different pictures of emotional expression to help the child learn to distinguish different feelings.

Expression: Develop a range of ways of showing how we are feeling, for example, painting, music, stories, etc.

Behavioural

Reward: Use a range of different rewards, eg. praise, tangibles, activities and check that they are rewarding to the child, ie. they increase the desired behaviour.

Shape: Reward the first small step towards the behaviour required. Gradually increase the steps towards the target goal. This will also ensure a sense of early success.

Model: Draw the child's attention to a child who has the skill. Emphasise the benefits of having the skill.

Cognitive

Problem solving: Teach them to stop, think, choose.

Goal setting: Set small, measurable, achievable, realistically timed goals (SMART)

Self-monitoring: Help the child to record every example of when he/she successfully learns a target skill.

Each of the techniques can be used to help a child learn skills essential for competency and resiliency.

Much of what we have discussed in this chapter is not new. We have always taught children those skills essential to cope with the challenges they will meet. The idea of a resilient child highlights the need for us to build into our work the skills that children need. Research has shown resiliency increases children's ability to cope as well as enhancing the quality of their lives,

> The resilient child is a happy child

Vulnerable children

As we continue to identify children who have special
educational needs', it is worth focusing on those children who
will be particularly vulnerable to feelings of powerlessness.
Children who face challenges, such as; learning disabilities,
physical and sensory disabilities, and emotional, behavioural
and social problems will benefit from a systematic programme
that enables them to possess the resiliency to cope with their
challenges. A sad fact that many still find hard to recognise or
accept is that the challenges that these children face are to a
large extent of our making, not theirs. Society is designed for
those who meet the accepted norm: in height, physical dexterity,
learning skills, visual and auditory acuity, etc. If anyone falls
beneath these norms, it is obvious that they will face handicaps.
Access to our world is built on basic assumptions. But, for many
of us, these assumptions are incorrect.

Examples:

⌘ If everything is at the right height I can reach.
⌘ If the work is broken down I can learn.
⌘ With sign language I can communicate as well as you.
⌘ With lifts and ramps I can go where I want.
⌘ With my dog I can see all that I need to.

Children do not ask for the challenges they face, they have them.
The challenge is to achieve. But, everyday folk and too many
professionals, are still dominated by the medical model. The
problem resides within the individual. Most children with
special educational needs have to come to terms with the loss of

their 'normality'. A resiliency programme should be a must for every child 'labelled' as having special educational needs. This would aim to:

- promote self-esteem
- to allow them to be a person in their own right
- develop assertiveness skills
- develop will power and self-determination
- change those systems which disempower them.

Children with a wide range of challenges can leave our educational system unprepared for the harsh realities of the world in which we live. Name calling is a fact of life; being talked over/not to, happens; being stared at is a reality; being offered pity and sympathy; not being involved in decision making and being treated as asexual, are all commonplace aspects of modern life.

As children move through both their own developmental challenges as well as the additional challenges we face them with, their self-image and confidence takes many knocks. These knocks develop emotional knocks within them which drains their energy and resources from fully achieving their potential. A resiliency programme would address those issues that are too often passed over lightly or ignored because of their sensitivity. We will not strengthen children's resiliency by ignoring these challenges. Such a programme could also challenge many of those myths that perpetuate inappropriate attitudes towards young people who face disabilities.

- ❖ Be strong
- ❖ Be thankful
- ❖ Be passive
- ❖ Be positive
- ❖ Be quiet

I suggest that every child who is assessed as having special educational needs is offered a resiliency programme. Such a programme would be a positive step towards recognising the added burdens placed upon them by a system that is going into tomorrow backwards.

References

Haggerty R, Sherrod L, Garmezy N, Rutter M, eds (1996) *Stress, Risk, & Resiliency in Children & Adolescents*. Cambridge University Press, Cambridge

Strayhorn J (1988) *The Competent Child*. The Guilford Press, New York

Goleman D (1996) *Emotional Intelligence*. Bloomsbury, London

7

Sexual development in young children

There is a normal process by which children develop both emotionally and sexually, taking place from infancy onwards. All children experience a range of emotions; sadness, anger and joy. They also experience delight through touching their own bodies. This interest usually coincides with the child's increased bowel and bladder control. Toddlers enjoy running around naked, they enjoy their body and are proud of it. This is entirely natural and is a key aspect in their desire to learn about themselves and others in the process of eventually becoming sexually mature adults.

Because children are naturally interested in their own bodies as well those of others, school staff need to understand that much of the sexual behaviour that takes place between children is normal. There is a danger for any kind of sexual behaviour to be labelled as 'signs of abuse' and we must be cautious about this reaction: 'He/she did what!!' Such responses can display our own ambivalent attitudes towards children's sexuality.

Facts

❖ By the age of thirteen it is expected that 40–85% of children will have engaged in some form of sexual behaviour.

❖ Natural sexual development in childhood is an information gathering process, so children will explore their own and each other's bodies.

❖ Children do this through play, such as games of 'mummies and daddies' and 'doctors and nurses'.

❖ Twenty per cent of eight-year-old girls show signs of starting puberty.

Sexual behaviour in children can often be a very difficult issue for schools and it can give rise to extreme emotional reactions in adults, ranging from over-reaction, under-reaction to not reacting at all.

None of these responses is helpful. It is important to feel confident enough to act, if you have concerns. This can be made possible if school staff feel supported by good information, sound reasoning and good practice.

Key points

❆ Not all sexual behaviour in children needs an adult response. The development of healthy emotional and sexual relationships between children is normal and to be expected.

❆ Inappropriate sexual behaviour in children must be dealt with in similar ways to all inappropriate behaviour, ie. to provide clear boundaries and to establish positive consequences for appropriate behaviour. Our aim should be to enable children to take control and change their behaviour with appropriate support.

❆ Some behaviour will need specialist help, but it is nearly always people who know the child well and have day-today contact, such as teachers and support staff, who will initially notice the behaviour. Your role is therefore vital.

⌘ At a personal level you may find some of the behaviour and language extremely distressing or difficult to tolerate. We all have our different personal limits and sensitivities. It is important to have a colleague who will discuss these matters professionally and/or personally to maintain your own well-being. It helps to talk.

Information gathering

Before deciding if a child's particular behaviour is a cause for concern, it is important to collect key information from those adults who best know the child. Too often, decisions are made and actions taken by adults about a child's sexual behaviour before enough information has been gathered.

Adults can sometimes over-react to a situation — often making matters worse — or, alternatively, do nothing because they are unsure of what action to take.

By taking time to obtain information and then analysing it, informed and rational decisions can be made.

Key information

(Below are some key indicative questions, you may well think of others that you would like to add.)

1   Describe the behaviour that is causing concern?
2   Is someone keeping a record of when and where the behaviour occurs?

3 Is there anyone else involved; if so, are they of a similar age?
4 Is there an element of force involved?
5 Are other children or parents complaining?
6 Could this behaviour be happening in secret?
7 Has there been a change in their schoolwork or attitude?
8 How does the child respond when the behaviour is discussed?

Once the information has been gathered it may become apparent that the behaviour is normal, natural play appropriate to the child and its age group, or there may be indications that there are reasons to be concerned and a need for further action. The sexual behaviour observed in children is likely to fall into a number of different groups. Depending on which group we believe the behaviour belongs to, can indicate the type of actions to be taken.

The groups are as follows:

- natural and healthy sexual play
- sexually reactive behaviour
- secretive children
- sexually abused children.

Natural and healthy sexual play

Children's play is characterised by its voluntary nature. The children are of similar age and size, of mixed gender, and usually friends. The play is lighthearted and spontaneous, giggly in nature — the children are embarrassed when caught. A broad range of behaviour is included but they will stop the behaviour if asked — at least in the sight of the adult. Interest in this type of play waxes and wanes as the children have numerous other activities which interest them.

Key questions

1 Are the children involved of a similar age?
2 Are they a mixed group of boys and girls?
3 Is the sexual behaviour part of a game, eg. 'doctors and nurses'?
4 Do they play other games together, eg. football, skipping, etc.?
6 Do all the children seem happy to be involved?
7 Do they seem embarrassed when an adult intervenes?

If you have answered **yes** to most of these questions, the sexual behaviour is probably normal.

Ideas

Children are exposed to sexual information from a wide range of resources, often under little adult supervision. It is natural for children to take an interest in the 'plumbing', and this is what sex education used to focus on. Today, more emphasis is correctly given to the relationship in which sexual behaviour occurs. Children who are naturally exploring their emerging sexuality may well benefit from additional sessions on sex education. In all likelihood this is the time when they are self-motivated to learn.

Sexually reactive children

These children are out of balance and they focus more on their
sexuality than their normally developing peers. If spoken to they
may well recognise that their behaviour is inappropriate and
welcome help. They will often feel shame, guilt and anxiety
about their behaviour. While this group might have been abused
they have often been over-exposed to sexual material: material
with which they are unable to cope. Their behaviour can be seen
as their attempt to cope with their confusion.

Key questions

1 Does the child display different emotions when compared
   to their peers. For example, are they ashamed, guilty or
   afraid where other children are embarrassed?
2 Have they been over-exposed to adult sexual material,
   videos and magazines?
3 Does the behaviour happen more often when the child is on
   their own?
4 Does the child approach adults in a sexual way?
5 Do they seem motivated to change their behaviour?
6 Do they display sexualised behaviour — behaving in ways
   too knowledgeable for a child of their age?

If you have answered **yes** to most of these questions, the sexual
behaviour is probably sexually reactive behaviour and may
indicate abuse of some kind. Such children may:

- lack adequate supervision
- live in a sexually liberal family

- have witnessed or be experiencing abuse.

Ideas

Discuss your concerns with your school's child protection co-ordinator. Keep good records. In a calm, non-judgemental way, provide clear boundaries. Seek professional support while maintaining a caring, normal and non-abusive environment for the child.

Children who abuse others

These children will often have behavioural problems at home and school with no outside interests and few secure friends. They lack problem-solving skills and have little impulse control. Their sexual behaviour is beyond developmentally appropriate play and their thoughts and actions are often pervaded by sexuality. These children can be impulsive, compulsive and aggressive in their behaviour. Coercion is **always** a factor. They seek out children who are vulnerable, easy to fool, bribe or force. Their victims will have no say in what happens. Most will have been victims of sexual abuse. Almost **all** will have witnessed extreme physical violence between their carers.

Key questions

1 Is the behaviour impulsive, compulsive and aggressive?
2 Is their sexual behaviour beyond what would be developmentally expected?

3   Are there younger or vulnerable children involved?
4   Has the child few meaningful friendships?
5   Have you tried to stop the behaviour with little success?
6   Does the child use force or coercion?

If you have answered **yes** to most of these questions, the sexual behaviour is probably abusive behaviour and almost certainly indicates abuse of some kind.

These children will:

- have difficulties in a number of areas in their lives
- require specialist support.

Ideas

⌘   Set clear boundaries for acceptable behaviour.
⌘   Develop a self-esteem booster programme.
⌘   Allow safe ways for the child to express their emotions.
⌘   Build in relaxation activities throughout the day, music, stories, etc.
⌘   Keep in close contact with the family and other agencies involved.
⌘   Keep good records.

Parental involvement

It is a legal requirement, wherever possible, to involve parents and carers and to work jointly with them. We do not advocate that parents be excluded from this process, but if there are concerns over abuse, how parents are to be included will need to be fully considered by the head teacher, the police, the child protection co-ordinator and social services. This is because the interests of the child and those of the family may not always be the same.

Reasonable parents will appreciate your genuine concern for the safety and welfare of children in their care.

> Always refer concerns to your school's child
> protection officer and handbook.

Self-esteem

The need to maintain a child's sense of value and well being is always important. It is such confidence that enables a child to risk learning and to cope with some of the everyday knocks that all children experience. But, when a child's sexual behaviour is giving cause for concern we can appreciate that they are likely to feel negative about themselves. A suggested idea for the 'Children who abuse others' group was to, 'develop a self-esteem booster programme'. Below are some ideas as to what exactly such a programme might look like.

A self-esteem booster programme

Positive thinking

Children, like adults, fall into thinking traps. They believe that because they did something wrong once, they will **always** do things wrong; because someone does not like them, they are unlikeable. The more such negative thoughts are rehearsed the stronger they become and the more readily they will enter a child's thoughts. They become, 'automatic negative thoughts'. To challenge these, help a child learn some 'automatic positive thoughts'. Teach them to remember such thoughts as:

- ⌘ One thing I do well is....
- ⌘ Three things I like about myself are....
- ⌘ I can always be relied on to....
- ⌘ A skill I have recently learned is....
- ⌘ My friends like me because....
- ⌘ A problem I recently overcome was....

These need not only be learned, but practised regularly.

Exercise

Regular exercise is not only good for the body, it is also good for the mind. During exercise, chemicals are released which give rise to a positive mood. (One of the best forms of exercise is dancing. It is physical, social and the music is uplifting.)

Target setting

Helping a child to set themselves realistic targets will strengthen a child's self-esteem through giving them a sense of achievement as well as personal competency: 'I can'.

Music

Help a child find pieces of music that they really enjoy. Top sports people often have an invigorating piece of music that they listen to in their mind before they perform. Such music can be associated with positive emotional memories and can be used as a trigger to help a child feel good in difficult situations.

Relaxation

Just like adults, children need time to relax and unwind. This may be in front of a TV soap. Other relaxing activities include:

- having a bath
- reading
- walking the dog
- playing football
- listening to music.

Friends

Friends are those people who cheer us up when we are down and with whom time flows quickly. A period spent in their company each day is essential.

Food

While we cannot ensure that children avoid excessive 'junk food' we can 'tell them, show them and let them', have access to healthy food. Each day the brain needs:

- oxygen — teach deep breathing
- water
- vitamins from vegetables
- exercise.

While the above are important as they strengthen a child's sense of personal value, the last ingredient — empathy — is the most significant. Without this, we will have children who care more about how they feel and not much about the feelings of others. True self-esteem means that not only 'I feel good, but I care also how "you" feel'.

Empathy

The more a child can describe how they feel about themselves — often in reaction to various events — the more you can help them understand that others feel similar in such circumstances as well. You may have to develop a range of emotional words to help them describe their internal world (*Chapter 2*).

A self-esteem booster programme means that rather than hoping a child is looking after how they feel we work out a set routine of activities that we know will help support them through what, for many, can be a distressing time.

Acknowledgement

This chapter is based on, *Sexual Behaviour in Primary Aged Children* written by Rob Long and Liz Morris (Long R, Morris L, 2002, Education Works, 4 Glendale Terrace, Castle Hill, totnes, Devon TQ9 5NY).

References

Cavanagh Johnson T (1991) *Understanding the Sexual behaviours of Young Children*. Siecus Report, South Pasadena, California

Lieberman A (1993) *The Emotional Life of the Toddler*. The Free Press, New York

8

Stress-proofing children

The stress of teaching is now widely acknowledged — new priorities and paperwork are neverending. But are schools equally stressful for children? We hear of children losing sleep because of their forthcoming SATs and other exams. Children face a wide range of challenges in school which is natural — schools are intended to be both stimulating and challenging. For many children, school is the beginning of their journey into the outside world. Until then, their lives are spent in the company of their immediate family and close friends. This is an informal, emotional context. The people around them respond quickly to their needs. Each child learns how to gain attention from the adults around in order to have needs met. When children arrive in school these ways may not always be the most appropriate. For example, waiting your turn may be a new experience, as may be sharing and listening. While many children have these skills, for some it is another area where they may not meet the expectations of the adults around them. Always remember that a strong motivator for children is the need to please significant adults. When children feel unable to do this they will experience psychological discomfort — stress.

Many children have the skills of being able to listen, co-operate, share, carry out instructions, but for some these will be skills they need to learn. Being faced with a range of new and different expectations is challenging for any child, but for some children it will be stressful. This type of stress is in reaction to an overload of demands.

Stress-proofing is intended to help children cope with their reactions to excessive demands, it is not intended to remove the natural responses children have to such family events as:

- family conflicts
- family separation
- bereavement.

Such events will make a child oversensitive to any demands or criticism in school. Feelings of anger and sadness are natural responses to such events as bereavement. The pain that follows is a healing pain.

Why are some children more prone to stress?

While each child has a different temperament, this interacts with the environment in which the child is raised. This inherited tendency combines with the strength of security that they attach to their carer/s. Children who have a secure attachment tend to be more sociable. Children who have a less secure attachment are more likely to have such difficulties as being isolated, hostile, fearful and anxious.

But stress can affect every child. Even a happy, secure and socially skilled child can become overwhelmed if too many demands are made of him/her. All children are prone to stress, but some children are more prone than others.

What is stress?

Pressure is what we experience when we have the skills to be able to cope with the challenges we face. When too many pressures come around at the same time this can trigger a stress reaction. Stress is what we experience when the load becomes too heavy. For children, the following can be a useful image:

> Imagine you are a little yellow truck. You can normally climb steep hills well. But one day you are overloaded and the effort needed now to climb the hill is too much. Under such conditions a range of negative feelings will be aroused, these will include feelings of anxiety, fear, lack of confidence, sadness as well as anger.

There are two aspects to stress. Firstly, there are the outside factors that **may** give rise to stress. Secondly, there are the responses that an individual **may** have. The key to whether or not stress will be experienced will depend on the child's perception of the situation. The model illustrates, with examples, how stress may or may not be experienced.

Threat	**Threat**
Being called names	Being called names
Appraisal	**Appraisal**
This is childish behaviour	I like these people
Coping skills	**Coping skills**
I can ignore them	I don't know what to do
Reaction	**Reaction**
No stress	Stress

How do children respond to stress?

When children are faced with excessive demands they respond in a number of ways. It is not uncommon for some children, boys especially, to act out their stress. This reaction often leads to their being reprimanded. Many children with behavioural difficulties are actually responding to stress in their lives.

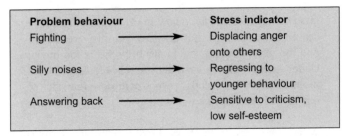

Problem behaviour		Stress indicator
Fighting	⟶	Displacing anger onto others
Silly noises	⟶	Regressing to younger behaviour
Answering back	⟶	Sensitive to criticism, low self-esteem

Stress can be seen as a normal response to circumstances that a child believes are not manageable. Life is not problem free and at some time in their school career all children will experience stress. What can we do about it? Stress-proofing is a realistic attempt to help children cope with the challenges that they will face. The earlier we can begin to teach children positive techniques, the better prepared they will be for the many challenges that they will inevitably face.

Are there any gender differences?

This is an interesting and difficult question to answer. We know that in schools the vast majority of children who display emotional, behavioural and social difficulties are boys. We know that women are more prone to depression than men. There are a range of factors that do act differently in boys and girls that would lead us to answer this question as more yes than no. This is not to deny that when we are talking about a specific individual the answer may be no.

Firstly, the hormonal differences between male and female increases the likelihood of boys acting out when faced with pressures (testosterone). Generally speaking, the physical size and strength differences between boys and girls makes acting out more likely again to occur in boys. Girls are more likely to talk through their stresses and to have a wider range of emotional reactions to stress. Put basically, girls prefer to talk about their feelings while boys prefer action and deeds. The fact that girls usually acquire language ahead of boys reinforces the tendency for girls to talk through feelings rather than acting them out.

Socially, these trends are reinforced by family and social roles and images. In school, boys' misbehaviour is more accepted as normal than the same behaviour in a girl. This can result in boys and girls developing different reactions and coping strategies to any stress that they face.

School stressors

Some possible stressors that children face in school, include:

- friendship conflicts
- learning failures
- changing classes
- pressure to succeed
- learning difficulties
- bullying.

School is potentially stressful in that it:

- expects children to master new understandings and skills
- expects the development of positive interpersonal relationships with adults and peers
- expects young people to give 100% in each lesson in which they take part.

Stress symptoms

⌘ Infantile behaviours — bed wetting, crying, nail biting, thumb sucking
⌘ Isolation — non-communicative behaviour
⌘ Eating problems
⌘ Physical symptoms — headaches, stomach upsets, sickness anxiety
⌘ Irritability
⌘ Relationship problems.

In fact, any change in a child's usual behaviour could be a reaction to stress.

The indicators of stress can be physical, psychological and behavioural. **It is always important when a child complains of physical symptoms that they are properly investigated by a nurse or doctor — stress is only one possible explanation.**

We cannot ensure that our children have problem free lives — this would make them less able to cope with the challenges that they will inevitably face, life is not problem free. Just as exposure to various germs helps a child develop a strong immune system, so coping with pressures will enable children to develop the necessary understanding and skills to manage stress effectively.

Stress-proofing programmes will contain three core elements:

> **Understanding ❖ Reactions ❖ Coping skills**

Understanding

The truck analogy is a simple but effective way to help children appreciate how they can only manage to do so much at any one time. Find out from the children the words that they use to describe their feelings in different negative situations. Make a 'word bank' of emotional words for them to use, eg. sad, frightened, tense, nervous, excited, bored, angry, anxious mad, confused.

Help children to understand that when they feel such negative feelings as anger, sadness or worry, that it is their body's way of telling them that things are not right and that they need to take some form of action. It can be reassuring to hear that your friends have similar experiences to you.

Teaching objectives

Children can:

- explain stress
- recognise stress in self and others
- understand causes of stress for themselves.

Reactions

Like adults, children vary in their response to stress. Symptoms will show in their behaviour, thinking, body (physiology) and feelings. (Because all children differ, one child might have a strong reaction in one area and a weak response in another.)

Faulty thinking

- ⌘ I must be liked by everyone.
- ⌘ Nobody ever likes me.
- ⌘ I must always do well.
- ⌘ I'm bad if I make mistakes.

Behaviours

- ⌘ Poor social skills.
- ⌘ Aggressive behaviour.
- ⌘ Stealing.

Body

- ⌘ Headaches.
- ⌘ Muscle tension.
- ⌘ Stomach upsets.

Feelings

- ⌘ Anger.
- ⌘ Sadness.
- ⌘ Anxiety.

Note that there are no direct techniques to change how we feel. We cannot just 'snap out of it'. However, the techniques for each of the other reactions; thinking, behaviour and body, will help improve how a child is feeling.

Teaching objective

Children can:

- explain the different reactions to stress.

Coping skills

A range of skills can be developed to help children deal with each of the above symptoms.

Body

Relaxation techniques can be taught to block such symptoms as rapid breathing and muscle tension. Children can be taught to breathe slowly and deeply. Tensing muscles and then relaxing them can similarly release the tension which builds up in their muscles. These can be incorporated into physical education (PE), dance or music lessons.

Thinking skills

Teaching children to have an 'I can' and 'I will' attitude can help challenge faulty thinking. Problem-solving skills will also enable them to have a range of options when they feel stuck.

Behaviour skills

Teaching children how to plan their time is a good stress management skill. How to be assertive is also another core skill in how to express yourself appropriately.

Life style skills would also be a core element of such a course teaching children the need for:

- a healthy diet
- exercise
- time with friends
- fun and relaxation.

Teaching objective

Children can:

- produce their own stress action plan.

Emotional literacy

It is worth noting that more and more schools are developing ways to support students emotional development. This is being achieved through promoting emotional literacy. Many of us have for a long time emphasised the need to include emotional understanding and skills into the curriculum. The pressure for this has received support from the popularisation of the work of Daniel Goleman. His book, *Emotional Intelligence*, has made explicit what many people had intuitively known for some time.

Too much emphasis has been placed on intelligence (IQ) and too little on emotions (emotional literacy [EQ]).

There are three core aspects to emotional literacy, and they each have a central role to play in developing stress management skills in young people.

Self-awareness

At its heart, EL seeks to help people identify their feelings and understand the different causes for them. An example would be that too often people believe that aggressive behaviour is caused by the internal emotion of anger. Anger is treated as a primary cause for the behaviour. But what caused the anger? Anger is often a secondary emotion. It can be caused through:

- loss and bereavement
- frustration at not being able to master a set task
- envy of what others have
- fear of failure
- rejection.

Emotional literacy helps learners to identify correctly different feelings and to recognise the causes for them. The more able they are to identify them correctly, the better able they will be to talk about and determine their causes. Without such skills, young people can be overwhelmed by their emotions. They can feel that they are abnormal or different because of the ways in which they are feeling.

Emotional management

Through an increased understanding of the nature and function of emotions, students are able to see that negative emotions can be carrying important information. Depending on the circumstances, it may be that:

- They are feeling sad because they have been separated from someone they care for.
- They feel angry because of an unexpected failure in a test.
- They feel lonely and isolated because they have not been invited to a party.

Through being able to understand the nature and reasons for the emotions, students are able to respond in more adaptive ways. Many negative emotions are not bad in themselves. Feeling sad or angry is often a healthy and justifiable response. How it is accepted and managed is the important thing

It is easy to see that these two areas are central to developing stress management skills in young people. In fact, these are skills that many adults could do well to learn. Stress can be used to energise us into action when we understand its dynamics. Without this we can too easily become its victims.

References

Support Groups for Children, Washington DC

O'Rourke K, Worzbyt JC (1996) *Accelerated Development*